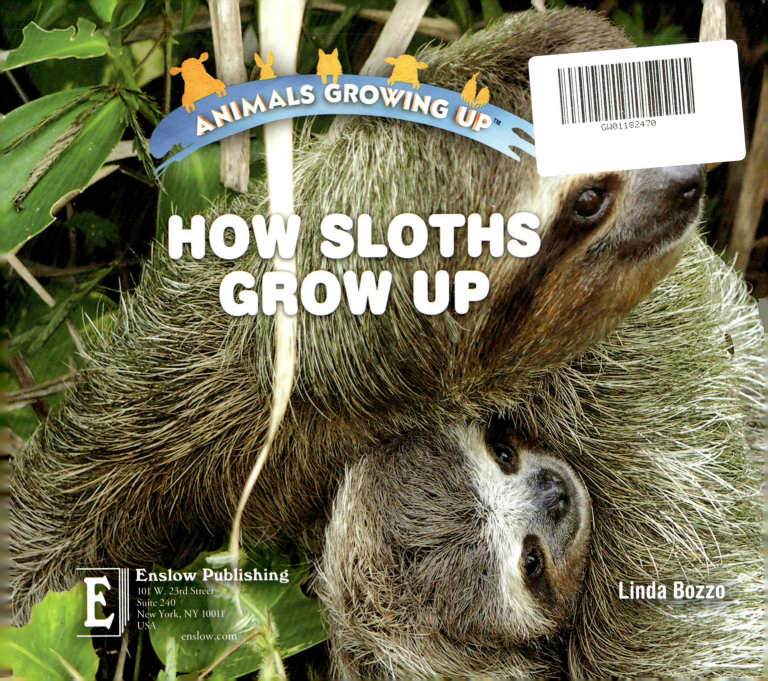

Animals Growing Up™

HOW SLOTHS GROW UP

Linda Bozzo

Enslow Publishing
101 W. 23rd Street
Suite 240
New York, NY 10011
USA

enslow.com

WORDS TO KNOW

algae Plantlike organisms without leaves or stems that grow in damp or wet places.

birds of prey Birds, such as eagles and owls, that hunt and eat other animals.

camouflage To hide by blending in with the surroundings.

cub A baby sloth.

mammals Warm-blooded animals that breathe air, have backbones and hair, and produce milk for their young.

nutrients Things found in food that give animals energy and help them grow.

predators Animals that kill and eat other animals to live.

rain forests Warm forests where a lot of rain falls.

weapons Things that can be used to fight against an attack.

CONTENTS

WORDS TO KNOW 2

BIRTH IN THE TREES 4

HOLD TIGHT 6

SAFE TO EAT 8

SAVING ENERGY 10

HANG IN THERE! 12

BATHROOM BREAK 14

SPEEDY SWIMMERS 16

FIGHTING BACK .18

WEARING GREEN 20

SLOWLY READY .22

LEARN MORE 24

INDEX 24

BIRTH IN THE TREES

Sloths are cute **mammals** that live in **rain forests**. They spend most of their time high above the ground in treetops. The mother sloth hangs upside down from the branches. Her baby is called a **cub**.

FAST FACT

There are two groups of sloths: two-toed sloths and three-toed sloths.

A three-toed sloth cub hangs out in its tree in Costa Rica. Costa Rica is a tropical country in Central America.

HOLD TIGHT

As soon as the sloth cub is born, it grabs hold of its mother's belly. They move through the trees together. Soon, the cub will be strong enough to travel on its own.

FAST FACT

The father sloth does not help the mother raise her baby.

A cub hangs onto its mother as they rest in the branches.

SAFE TO EAT

Sloth cubs drink their mother's milk for the first few weeks. As the cub grows, it also starts to eat leaves. It learns from its mother which leaves are safe to eat.

FAST FACT

Sometimes sloths eat fruit, flowers, and bugs, too.

A sloth cub eats leaves upside down in its rain forest home.

SAVING ENERGY

Sloth cubs do not get many **nutrients** from their diets. Nutrients are things found in food that give animals energy and help them grow. Cubs must rest most of the day to save energy.

FAST FACT

Sloths have long tongues to pull leaves into their mouths.

A two-toed sloth cub slowly climbs along a branch in Costa Rica.

HANG IN THERE!

A sloth cub can sleep and eat hanging upside down. But sloths spend most of their time sleeping! Sometimes they curl up in a ball to snooze.

FAST FACT

Sloth cubs are born with long curved claws.

A cub sleeps as it holds onto the branch with its claws.

BATHROOM BREAK

About once a week, the sloth cub slowly comes down from the trees. It needs a bathroom break! After it is done, it must climb back up into the trees where it is safe.

FAST FACT

Sloths are very slow on the ground. It is dangerous for them to be there.

A two-toed sloth cub crawls along the forest floor. It must find its way back up into the trees before it is spotted by a hungry animal.

SPEEDY SWIMMERS

Sloth cubs move slowly on the ground. But they move fast in the water. They drop from trees into rivers. SPLASH! Sloths use their long arms to swim well.

FAST FACT

Sloths are the slowest mammals in the world.

A pygmy three-toed sloth swims in Panama. Panama is next to Costa Rica.

FIGHTING BACK

Sloth cubs have their mothers to keep them safe. A mother sloth uses her curved claws and sharp teeth as **weapons** to fight off **predators**. Wild cats and some kinds of **birds of prey** hunt sloths.

A pale-throated three-toed sloth protects her cub. She will do whatever it takes to stop predators from hurting her baby.

FAST FACT

Harpy eagles are a sloth's greatest enemy.

WEARING GREEN

Tiny, green plant-like organisms called **algae** grow on the sloth's fur. This helps sloths **camouflage** themselves from danger. They blend in with the tree leaves. Predators can't see them.

FAST FACT

Sloths do not run. They must stay quiet and still to stay safe.

A mother and cub's green fur matches the leaves. They are almost invisible to predators.

SLOWLY READY

After a year or so, the sloth cub is ready to leave its mother. The cub will not travel far. It finds trees of its own nearby where it will live.

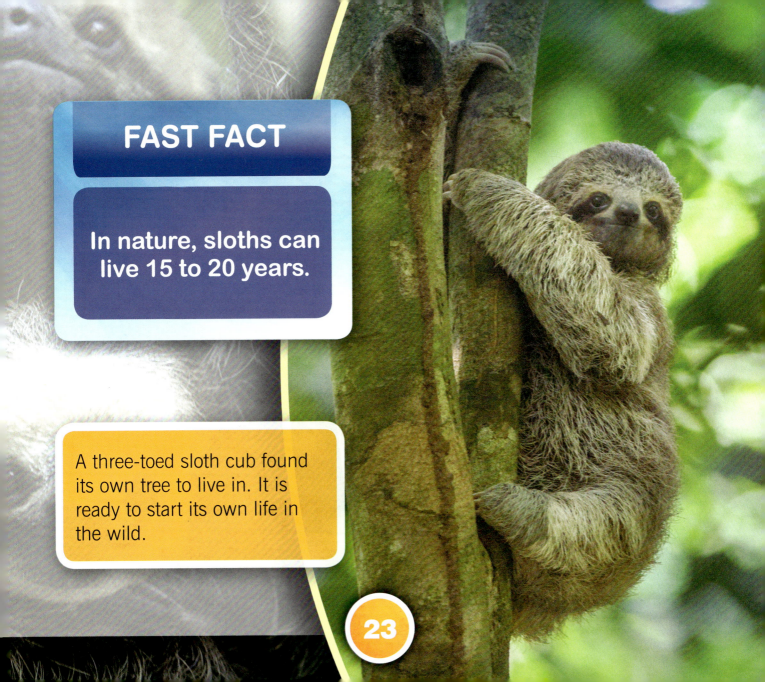

FAST FACT

In nature, sloths can live 15 to 20 years.

A three-toed sloth cub found its own tree to live in. It is ready to start its own life in the wild.

LEARN MORE

Books

Bodden, Valerie. *Sloths*. Mankato, MN: Creative Education, 2018.

DK. *Sloths*. New York: DK Publishing, 2019.

Murray, Julie. *Sloths*. Minneapolis, MN: Abdo Kids, 2017.

Websites

National Geographic Kids: Sloth
kids.nationalgeographic.com/animals/sloth/
Read fun facts about sloths.

San Diego Zoo Kids: Two-Toed Sloth
kids.sandiegozoo.org/animals/two-toed-sloth
Learn about the special features of the two-toed sloth.

INDEX

claws, 13, 18
Costa Rica, 5, 11, 17
diet, 10
fur, 20
ground, 4, 15, 16
leaves, 8, 9, 11, 20, 21
mother, 4, 6, 7, 8, 18, 21, 22
Panama, 17
predators, 18, 19, 20, 21
rain forest, 4, 9
sleep, 12, 13
teeth, 18
three-toed sloth, 5, 17, 19, 23
tongue, 11
travel, 6, 22
trees, 6, 14, 15, 16, 22
two-toed sloth, 5, 11, 15
water, 16

Published in 2020 by Enslow Publishing, LLC
101 W. 23rd Street, Suite 240, New York, NY 10011

Copyright © 2020 by Enslow Publishing, LLC

All rights reserved.

No part of this book may be reproduced by any means without the written permission of the publisher.

Library of Congress Cataloging-in-Publication Data

Names: Bozzo, Linda, author.
Title: How sloths grow up / Linda Bozzo.
Description: New York : Enslow Publishing, 2020. | Series: Animals growing up | Audience: K to Grade 3. | Includes bibliographical references and index.
Identifiers: LCCN 2019007725 | ISBN 9781978512436 (library bound) | ISBN 9781978512412 (paperback) | ISBN 9781978512429 (6 pack)
Subjects: LCSH: Sloths—Development—Juvenile literature. | Sloths—Infancy—Juvenile literature.
Classification: LCC QL737.E2 B69 2020 | DDC 599.3/13—dc23
LC record available at https://lccn.loc.gov/2019007725

Printed in the United States of America

To Our Readers: We have done our best to make sure all website addresses in this book were active and appropriate when we went to press. However, the author and the publisher have no control over and assume no liability for the material available on those websites or on any websites they may link to. Any comments or suggestions can be sent by email to customerservice@enslow.com.

Photos Credits: Cover, p. 1 Kristel Segeren/Shutterstock.com; interior pages 4-23 (background), p. 7 MMPOP/Shutterstock.com; p. 5 Damsea/Shutterstock.com; p. 9 J_K/Shutterstock.com; p. 11 John & Lisa Merrill/Photodisc/Getty Images; p. 13 Akkharat Jarusilawong/Shutterstock.com; p. 15 Kristel Segeren/Shutterstock.com; p. 17 Bill Hatcher/National Geographic Image Collection/Getty Images; p. 19 Robert E. Barber/Alamy Stock Photo; p. 21 gabriele brentegani/Shutterstock.com; p. 23 Mark Downey/Corbis Documentary; back cover and additional interior pages background graphic 13Imagery/Shutterstock.com